Sanctuary

In the Secret Place

H. L. Robertson

No part of this publication may be reproduced, stored in a retrieval system or transmitted in any way by any means, electronic, mechanical, photocopying, recording, or otherwise without the prior permission of the author except as provided by USA copyright law.

Scripture quotations are taken from the Holy Bible, King James version, Cambridge, 1769. Used by permission. All rights reserved.

Book design copyright 2017 Fairhaven Media. All rights reserved.

Cover design by Izzit Graphics

Interior design by H L Robertson

Published in the United States of America

1. Religion/Biblical Criticism & Interpretation/General

2. Religion/Biblical Commentary/ General

16.03.31

ISBN: 978-1-947729-01-8

To Dr. Dwain Miller whose teachings on Jesus as a Rabbi have revolutionized my view of the Gospels

Table of Contents

Introduction		9
Chapter One	The Secret Place	19
Chapter Two	Under His Wings	29
Chapter Three	The Tallit	39
Chapter Four	Entering In	53
Chapter Five	The Wedding Canopy	61
Chapter Six	The Bride is Betrothed	67
Chapter Seven	The Holiest Place	81
Chapter Eight	Abiding	91
Chapter Nine	The Tabernacle of David	99

6

He that dwelleth in the secret place of the most High shall abide under the shadow of the Almighty.
Psalms 91:1

8

Introduction

He that dwelleth in the secret place of the most High shall abide under the shadow of the Almighty. I will say of the LORD, He is my refuge and my fortress: my God; in him will I trust. Psalms 91:1-2

Psalm 91 is perhaps the single most widely read, and quoted, scripture passage concerning divine protection. It is, in fact, 'stock in trade' for virtually any preacher, teacher, commentator, or writer dealing with the subject. Verses one and two in particular are not only quoted with great frequency, but are inscribed on plaques, bookmarks, Christian artwork, and other paraphernalia. In this book we will examine these verses in detail. However, along with Psalm 91, I also want to look at another tremendously rich and informative passage from the Psalms that sadly is largely overlooked. Psalm 27 goes into much more detail about the actual subject of God's sanctuary and His place of protection; so that between the two passages we can piece together a much more comprehensive picture of this vitally important covenant promise than either can give by itself.

Let's start by examining Psalm 91 and dig into some essential word studies on the Hebrew terms used in this passage. At the very beginning of Psalm 91:1 we encounter the word 'dwelleth'. The Hebrew word used here is 'yashab'. It is important to understand that this word doesn't simply refer to the place that someone lives; but it infers a dwelling place of a person involved in the temple ministry. This place would be in, or at the least, very near to the temple. This gives us a picture of God's intentions for us to be in close fellowship with Him and intimately involved in His worship and service. Just as those ancient priests and Levites could not possibly minister in the Holy Temple while living far away; we must develop and maintain a close relationship with Father God if we are to serve and minister before Him. This word is also used in an interesting passage that may be a little surprising to some readers. It is found in Psalm 65:4, the passage used as a basis for part of the Jewish circumcision ritual!

Blessed is the man whom thou choosest, and causest to approach unto thee, that he may dwell in thy courts: we shall be satisfied with the goodness of thy house, even of thy holy temple. Psalms 65:4

Once again we see that our heavenly father fully intends for us to live life 'up close and personal' with Him from our very beginnings. The circumcision ceremony is performed on a newborn baby boy's eighth day. Eight is the biblical number representing a new beginning and represents the genesis of an existence carried out in covenant with God and under His authority and blessing. From a medical viewpoint it is the singular day in a male's life when the vitamin K and prothrombin (clotting factors) are at their absolute peak; sustaining a level that will never be repeated in that individual's lifetime; spiking to a point significantly above the normal maximum levels. Here at the very inception of the spiritual journey with the Lord, we see Lord's abundant and omniscient provision for His people.

The next key word in these verses is 'luwn' (abide). Luwn means to dwell, abide or remain. While 'yashab' has a connotation of permanence, 'luwn' infers a temporary accommodation; an overnight lodging; a place of sojourning. In fact it is the modern Hebrew word used for a hotel. This points out the fact that God doesn't intend for us to huddle behind His throne, but to walk in freedom and a relationship of fellowship, with the understanding that He will be our sheltering place when trials come. This is reinforced by the next two words we will look at: 'machaleh' which is translated refuge; and 'matsund' which is rendered fortress.

Machaleh implies a place of refuge and shelter from adverse circumstances such as rain, storms, or any such natural danger. Matsund on the other hand represents a fortress or castle which affords complete protection from all enemy attacks to its occupants. These two words, which at first glance seem to be synonyms, are actually showing two distinct facets of God's protection.

Notice that the very first word we examined: yashab refers to a place where we actually live on a continuing, day-to-day basis. Machaleh and matsund point to places of protection in adverse life situations that are both natural and demonically spawned. The persons implied by yashab were, as stated previously, in the temple worship and service. They did not live in the temple proper but in apartments in or near the temple complex. By the same token we cannot carry on our spiritual lives within the walls of our churches. Similarly, in the agricultural society these verses were written to, people could not simply take up permanent residence in the refuge or fortress; they had to carry out their occupation outside the walls raising crops and/or tending their flocks.

To further delve into these ideas let's look at Psalm 27 now.

One thing have I desired of the LORD, that will I seek after; that I may dwell in the house of the LORD all the days of my life, to behold the beauty of the LORD, and to enquire in his temple. For in the time of trouble he shall hide me in his pavilion: in the secret of his tabernacle shall he hide me; he shall set me up upon a rock. Psalms 27:5

Once again it is important to remember that the word 'dwell' here is 'yashab' which carries the connotation of permanence. What we are seeing is a description of a continual relationship and fellowship with periodic, regularly occurring encounters of a deeper, more meaningful nature. This concept is carried on with the next two words we will look at: 'behold' and 'enquire'.

The Hebrew word translated 'behold' is the word 'chazah' which means to behold or see as a seer. This word describes a profound, even prophetic, encounter of a revelatory nature. We must remember that King David was gifted not only as a psalmist, but penned a tremendous volume of scriptures which were deeply prophetic. This is especially true of his Messianic passages. David is describing to us his desire to experience an episode that transcended worship, one that involved an impartation to himself from God. The meaning of 'chazah' stands in a clear and direct contrast to the Hebrew word translated 'enquire'. The Hebrew verb 'baqar' used here refers to seeking with pleasure or delight. It describes a fellowship encounter in which both participants are enjoying the presence of the other party. Here Psalm 27 gives us a picture of a lifestyle of intimacy in which the worshipper and God had an ongoing relationship which consisted of a balanced blend of shared fellowship and received spiritual impartation.

It is important to also note that verse 5 shows us 'baqar' used in relation to the temple or 'heykel' in Hebrew. The temple was the appointed place for the connection of heaven with earth in the embodiment of God's manifest presence; i.e. the 'Shekinah' glory cloud. (see my book Bring in the Glory for more on this subject) This indicates that in David's time there was a special importance and emphasis placed on the temple as a venue for meeting with God. The Apostle Paul admonishes us in Hebrews 10:25 against "forsaking assembling of ourselves together". By contrast, 1 Corinthians 6:19 tells us that we (our bodies) are "the temple of the Holy Ghost". This indicates that while the New Covenant makes our spirit man the repository of God's indwelling presence in the person of the Holy Spirit, we are still under a mandate to meet together with other believers regularly in a corporate setting. This in direct contrast to 'chazah' which is a personal and oftentimes deeply private episode between just the worshipper and the Lord. This is reminiscent of Jesus instruction in Matthew 6:6 to "enter into thy closet". The concept of the closet both in surface meaning and inference is almost identical to that of the 'secret place' in Psalm 91. (more on this in chapter one) We see then that while the 'beholding' is generally a private, introspective experience; the 'enquiring' is just the opposite: an open, inclusive fellowship event in which sharing and interacting with other believers is not only encouraged, but required.

Psalm 27 verse five introduces another important word: 'pavilion'. The Hebrew word here is 'cok'. This word is a derivative of the word 'cakak' which literally means to hedge in, defend, or cover. Once again we see the implied covering of protection provided in our covenant relationship. 'Cok' is also the root word of 'sukkah' or 'booths' from which we get the word 'Sukkot' or the festival of booths. The 'sukkah' or booth was a temporary dwelling intended to remind Israel of their forefathers who lived in temporary dwellings as they wandered in the wilderness for forty years. This reiterates the idea of the transient nature of the place of God's refuge and protection: it's there when needed, not a permanent dwelling to shut oneself off from the world. Jesus himself highlighted this principle when he said:

I pray not that thou shouldest take them out of the world, but that thou shouldest keep them from the evil. John 17:15

The final word to examine in this passage is the word translated 'tabernacle' which is 'ohel'. This Hebrew word means a dwelling tent such as the Bedouin used. It was also used for the original "tabernacle" that Moses constructed outside the Hebrews' camp in which he met with God. This word was not used, however, of the

Tabernacle of Moses which housed the ark of the covenant and was constructed only after the Israelites rejected a personal relationship with God at Mount Sinai. This seems to be an intentional distinction. The original tabernacle Moses built, like the tabernacle of David many generations later was a place for meeting God in a first hand, unfettered manner. This was the very first earthly 'sanctuary'!

Chapter One

He that dwelleth in the secret place of the most High shall abide under the shadow of the Almighty. I will say of the LORD, He is my refuge and my fortress: my God; in him will I trust. Surely he shall deliver thee from the snare of the fowler, and from the noisome pestilence. He shall cover thee with his feathers, and under his wings shalt thou trust: his truth shall be thy shield and buckler. Thou shalt not be afraid for the terror by night; nor for the arrow that flieth by day; Nor for the pestilence that walketh in darkness; nor for the destruction that wasteth at noonday. A thousand shall fall at thy side, and ten thousand at thy right hand; but it shall not come nigh thee. Psalms 91:1-7

Psalm 91 verses one and two contain some of the most beautiful and poetic language in the entire Bible. One phrase in particular, which has captured the imagination of millions, is the words 'secret place' from verse one. The Hebrew word here is 'cethar' which means a secret place or hiding place. This word is derived from the word 'cathar' which means to hide or conceal. The Introduction discusses the implications of the word 'dwell' and its association with those who live in or near the temple complex. These two ideas joined together give us further insight into the concept that 'dwelling' yields protection. A close spiritual proximity to God produces the best opportunity for His intervention in our life circumstances. Let me reiterate that this scenario doesn't mean we are to hole up in some sort of a permanent spiritual refuge. God doesn't want spiritual hermits! We are clearly instructed to occupy until he returns according to Luke 19:13. It does, however, give us a glimpse of the manner of life we should conduct; especially when we understand the pastoral type of existence the Jewish people carried on in Bible times.

The Holy Land is littered with mounds or 'tells' which are ruined remnants of ancient cities. These cities were, almost without exception, fortified in some manner to protect their citizens from the depredations of marauding bands of soldiers: from bona fide enemy nations, or just plain freelance bandits who picked on targets of opportunity. The majority of the people lived not in but around these small, many times, independent cities. They raised their crops, carried out their trades, and tended their animals in order to provide or barter for the commodities they needed to sustain life. This was all carried out 'under the protection' of the city walls. In time of attack watchmen on the walls sounded a warning and the people would flee to the fortified city for protection and to participate in the mutual defense efforts of the citizenry. The people would also carry or herd as much of their harvest and livestock as possible into the confines of the city. After all, if one survived the attack only to starve to death later, all their heroic defense efforts were tragically wasted. This reinforces once again the principle that the city of refuge is a temporary respite from enemy attack, but the individual's life's work (not to mention their efforts toward material increase) is to be carried on outside the walls. This ideal is sadly lost on many modern churches, which tend many times to resemble a sort of spiritual frat house where believers go to hang out with their friends; more than a military outpost of God's kingdom where they are equipped to go out and do battle. Historically, a city's occupants only stayed within the walls to fight if they were overpowered, besieged, and cut off from outside help. We are in no such position; we are promised to be protected within God's secret place with the King and Creator of the universe as our defender!

The notion of a secret or hidden place is also found in Psalm 27. Verse five refers to the 'secret' (cethar) of His tabernacle. The psalmist goes on to describe God as setting him on a rock. The Hebrew word here 'ruwm' which means to exalt or set on high, and says he will do so 'on a rock', which in Hebrew means a cliff or rocky pinnacle. This implies a strong towering place that is sheltered from, and inaccessible to, our enemies. The analogy becomes crystal clear when one looks at the tells in Israel; nearly all were built elevated on high ground that commanded a wide view of the surrounding territory, were difficult to approach, and were strategically located near a water source; to make them in all ways as secure from enemy attack as possible. The Hebrew word construction provides a sort of encoding of these principles. The word translated 'abide' in Psalm 91: 'luwn' can be transformed into the word for 'set on high' – 'ruwm' by changing only two letters. The first letter in luwn: 'lamed' means has a word picture attached of learning. Let's change that letter for the first letter in ruwm: the Hebrew letter 'resh' which has a word picture of head or chief. Now take the last letter in luwn: the Hebrew letter 'nun' which has a word picture of faithfulness. Now, change that letter to the last letter in ruwm: the Hebrew letter 'mem' which has a word picture of water.

Begin with: luwn = abide

lamed = learning >> resh = head or chief

nun = faithfulness >> mem = water

Yields: ruwm = set on high

Thus we in transforming 'luwn' into 'ruwm' we have a process described for us in which learning God's will and ways added to our faithfulness in relationship to Him yields a chief place with water. This is exactly the defensive scenario described above! Once again, we see that abiding in fellowship with Him brings protection.

This is the kind of protection God is not only offering, but promising to His children. The key point to note here is that the promise is provisional. A family that lived on their own, far from a protecting city was easy game for attackers. Only by dwelling in fellowship and community with others was there a hope of protection. As believers, our position of protection is directly related to our continuing fellowship and relationship with Him.

The beginnings of this system of divine protection originated with the Israelites during the exodus from Egypt:

And they took their journey from Succoth, and encamped in Etham, in the edge of the wilderness. And the LORD went before them by day in a pillar of a cloud, to lead them the way; and by night in a pillar of fire, to give them light; to go by day and night: He took not away the pillar of the cloud by day, nor the pillar of fire by night, from before the people... And the angel of God, which went before the camp of Israel, removed and went behind them; and the pillar of the cloud went from before their face, and stood behind them: And it came between the camp of the Egyptians and the camp of Israel; and it was a cloud and darkness to them, but it gave light by night to these: so that the one came not near the other all the night.   Ex 13:20-22; 14:19-20

Here we see God's presence as both guide and protector. Particularly notice that the pillar of cloud and fire was a separating barrier from the Egyptians but that it also gave light by night to the Israelites. Once again we see that God is both protector and provider. This narrative continues throughout the forty years journey through the wilderness. The plan of their encampment as given by the

Lord to Moses, placed the tabernacle with the pillar of cloud (God's presence) in the center with the tribes encamped extending out north, south, east, and west from its central position. This symbolizes the fact that God intended that he alone was not only the center of their existence, but also that He would be their covering and protection rather than the fortifications of some walled city. In fact, the first city they were told to conquer was Jericho, the strongest walled city in the entire land of Canaan. It was considered impregnable to attack, but its walls were of no use whatsoever in the face of God's supernatural destruction. This was an object lesson to the Israelites that no walled city could serve as protection against God; and God alone was worthy to be trusted as their protector.

A further careful study of the tribes and their relative sizes will show that the resulting arrangement of the Israelites' camp formed a cross! Here is the promise for future believers that God will continue to fulfill those roles under the covenant that would be instituted with Christ's death on the cross, His burial, and His resurrection. Jesus himself hinted at this when he said in John 17:

And now I am no more in the world, but these are in the world, and I come to thee. Holy Father, keep through thine own name those whom thou hast given me, that they may be one, as we are. While I was with them in the world, I kept them in thy name: those that thou gavest me I have kept, and none of them is lost… John 17:11-12

The Greek word here for keep is 'tereo' which means to keep, hold, watch over, and preserve. When God chose to dwell in the spirit man of believers in the person of the Holy Spirit, he placed Himself not only in proximity to, but at ground zero of the fight with our enemy the devil. What better place to watch over something than from within! 1Corinthians 6:19 tells us that we are the 'temple of the Holy Ghost'. The Greek word here for temple is 'naos' meaning 'sanctuary' from the root word 'naio' which means to dwell. Since we know that God dwells in the heavenly temple; here we see the connection of heaven to earth through the Holy Spirit dwelling within in us. This revelation unveils the culmination of God's great mystery:

… Whereby, when ye read, ye may understand my knowledge in the mystery of Christ) Which in other ages was not made known unto the sons of men, as it is now revealed unto his holy apostles and propents by the Spirit… And to make all men see what is the fellowship of the mystery, which from the beginning of the world hath been hid in God, who created all things by Jesus Christ… Eph 3:4-9

The Apostle Paul is revealing to us this mystery; that just as the mystery of His future plan and will was hidden in Christ, we are now hidden in Him. All creation is made by Him, reconciled by His sacrifice on the cross, and now as many as receive the benefit of that sacrifice by faith are gathered into Him spiritually in this present world; and physically and eternally in the world to come. Paul shows us in 1 Corinthians 8 the unity which Christ has brought between the Trinity and redeemed creation:

But to us there is but one God, the Father, of whom are all things, and we in him; and one Lord Jesus Christ, by whom are all things, and we by him. 1 Cor 8:6

Notice in Ephesians 1 we are told that he purposed to 'gather' all things in Christ:

Having made known unto us the mystery of his will, according to his good pleasure which he hath purposed in himself: That in the dispensation of the fulness of times he might gather together in one all things in Christ, both which are in heaven, and which are on earth; even in him… Eph 1:9-10

Through these passages we see the theme develop. Words like 'hidden', 'in Him', and 'gather all' paint a picture of the New Testament correlation to the 'secret place' described by David in the Psalms. In fact, the Hebrew word for 'hide' in Psalm 27:5: 'tsaphan' means to treasure up or lie hidden. This is a wonderful picture in which David, by inspiration of the Spirit, is foretelling the secret, hidden, dwelling place God has created within His children.

Chapter Two

He that dwelleth in the secret place of the most High shall abide under the shadow of the Almighty. I will say of the LORD, He is my refuge and my fortress: my God; in him will I trust. Surely he shall deliver thee from the snare of the fowler, and from the noisome pestilence. He shall cover thee with his feathers, and under his wings shalt thou trust: his truth shall be thy shield and buckler. Psalms 91:1-4

As we examine our text once again a word jumps out at us; that word is 'shadow'. James tells us in his epistle: "Every good gift and every perfect gift is from above, and cometh down from the Father of lights, with whom is no variableness, neither shadow of turning" (James 1:17); and yet here we are confronted with a scripture that clearly describes us as being "under His shadow". This seems to present a contradiction until we understand the Hebrew word used in our text. The word 'shadow' is translated from the Hebrew word 'tsel'. Tsel has a connotation of covering; even defense. Psalm 91:1 is not conveying the idea that God produces, or in fact can produce darkness. It is reiterating the idea that we are covered over and protected by the Almighty.

Verse four confirms this meaning by the use of two Hebrew words utilized in tandem to focus our attention on the core truth of God's covering and protection for His children. The word 'feathers' is from the Hebrew 'ebrah' which could more perfectly be rendered 'wings' referring to actual pinions of a bird's wings. The second word is 'wings' which is from the Hebrew 'kanaph'. Kanaph is from a Hebrew root meaning literally 'to be put in a corner'. Kanaph emphasizes the space under the wings more so than the wings themselves. This is reinforced by the meaning of 'shadow' as discussed in the previous paragraph. These words gives us a picture of the workings of God's protective covering: He places us underneath His protective covering or 'shadow', and we in turn can fully 'trust' and rely on that protection.

These two Hebrew words: ebrah and kanaph are used together again, showing the contrast in their meaning, in Deuteronomy chapter 32:

When the most High divided to the nations their inheritance, when he separated the sons of Adam, he set the bounds of the people according to the number of the children of Israel. For the LORD'S portion is his people; Jacob is the lot of his inheritance. He found him in a desert land, and in the waste howling wilderness; he led him about, he instructed him, he kept him as the apple of his eye. As an eagle stirreth up her nest, fluttereth over her young, spreadeth abroad her wings, taketh them, beareth them on her wings: So the LORD alone did lead him, and there was no strange god with him. Deut 32:8-12

In this picture we are shown a mother eagle caring for her young. she 'spreadeth abroad her wings' – kanaph, and 'beareth them on her wings' – ebrah; once again differentiating between the actual process of protection and provision, and the place of protection and provision. The Lord also gave the Israelites an object lesson and constant reminder of these principles when He had them build the ark of the covenant. Exodus chapter 25 describes the ark and the cherubim which were on the cover or 'mercy seat'.

And thou shalt put into the ark the testimony which I shall give thee… And thou shalt make two cherubims of gold, of beaten work shalt thou make them, in the two ends of the mercy seat... And the cherubims shall stretch forth their wings on high, covering the mercy seat with their wings, and their faces shall look one to another; toward the mercy seat shall the faces of the cherubims be. And thou shalt put the mercy seat above upon the ark; and in the ark thou shalt put the testimony that I shall give thee. And there I will meet with thee, and I will commune with thee from above the mercy seat, from between the two cherubims which are upon the ark of the testimony… Ex 25:16-22

The wings of the cherubim covered the mercy seat as a sign of God's protective covering of His people. Notice also that the 'testimony' was to be placed inside. This testimony consisted of the tablets of stone, the golden pot of manna, and Aaron's rod which had budded. These items represented the nation of Israel's covenant relationship with God and were a reminder that as long as they remained in covenant they were covered under His wings of protection. He promised to meet with them from above the cherubim; showing that the covenant (and by inference we ourselves) were under the wings of His covering.

We get another beautiful picture of this ideal of God's covering in the story of Ruth and Boaz, and their budding romance. Ruth doesn't fully comprehend where she stands spiritually and yet receives the benefit of a covenant she doesn't understand or even have a working knowledge of.

Then she fell on her face, and bowed herself to the ground, and said unto him, Why have I found grace in thine eyes, that thou shouldest take knowledge of me, seeing I am a stranger? And Boaz answered and said unto her, It hath fully been shewed me, all that thou hast done unto thy mother in law since the death of thine husband: and how thou hast left thy father and thy mother, and the land of thy nativity, and art come unto a people which thou knewest not heretofore. The LORD recompense thy work, and a full reward be given thee of the LORD God of Israel, under whose wings thou art come to trust. Ruth 2:10-12

Ruth has come from the land of Moab, a country of pagan idol worshippers, and has through marriage been initiated into the worship of the one true God. After the death of her husband, father-in-law, and brother-in-law; Ruth goes to Israel with her mother-in-law Naomi. Here she encounters Boaz who eventually fulfills the law of Levirate marriage by taking Ruth as his wife and raising children to stand in their father's inheritance. This is a wonderful living lesson in our relationship to God. We, as fallen human beings, are separated from God in sin and unbelief, just as Ruth was as a Moabite living outside covenant with the Lord. We then see a picture of our salvation and entrance into God's kingdom as she believes in God, 'under whose wings (kanaph) thou art come to trust', and goes to live in Israel. She then comes under the covering and provision of her new husband Boaz which represents our coming under God's protection and provision in our covenant with Him through Jesus (the church's 'bridegroom' according to Matthew 9:15).

King David, who was Ruth and Boaz' great-grandson, penned a beautiful description of the benefits of God's covenant in Psalm 36:

How excellent is thy lovingkindness, O God! therefore the children of men put their trust under the shadow of thy wings. Psalms 36:7

Here once again appear the now familiar words shadow – tsel, and wings – kanaph. David tells us we can put our trust in Him but he now introduces a new word: lovingkindness. This is the Hebrew word 'chesed'. Chesed is a complex word that is rendered in various ways according to the translation; including lovingkindness, mercy, and grace. It has a sense of 'strength' and 'steadfastness'. These interwoven meanings lead us to understand David's statement in verses eight through ten that we can not only trust in His protection but rest in His great provision.

They shall be abundantly satisfied with the fatness of thy house; and thou shalt make them drink of the river of thy pleasures. For with thee is the fountain of life: in thy light shall we see light. O continue thy lovingkindness unto them that know thee; and thy righteousness to the upright in heart. Psalm 36:8-10

These scriptures depict an overflowing supply of God's blessings that issue forth from the place of His guarding shelter. David proceeds to tell us in Psalm 57 that the shadow of His wings will be our refuge. Notice once again that this concept of refuge is a temporary one: 'until these calamities be overpast'.

Be merciful unto me, O God, be merciful unto me: for my soul trusteth in thee: yea, in the shadow of thy wings will I make my refuge, until these calamities be overpast. Psalms 57:1

The word translated refuge here is 'chacah' which means to seek a refuge or hiding place. This indicates clearly that God's protection is available, but that we must actively participate in the covenant relationship and seek refuge in His shelter. This principle is shown again in Psalm 63:

When I remember thee upon my bed, and meditate on thee in the night watches. Because thou hast been my help, therefore in the shadow of thy wings will I rejoice. My soul followeth hard after thee: thy right hand upholdeth me. Psalms 63:6-8

The writer expresses his fervor in his relationship with the Lord: 'remember thee' and 'meditate on thee'. He then reiterates the familiar theme: 'in the shadow (tsel) of thy wings (kanaph) but goes on to state that his 'soul followeth hard after thee' indicating an all-consuming zeal for God's presence. In fact, the word translated 'followeth hard' is the Hebrew word 'dabaq' which means literally 'to stick to' and is the basis for the Hebrew word for glue!

Psalm 61 culminates this line of thought by presenting a wonderfully comprehensive depiction of all these concepts:

Hear my cry, O God; attend unto my prayer. From the end of the earth will I cry unto thee, when my heart is overwhelmed: lead me to the rock that is higher than I. For thou hast been a shelter for me, and a strong tower from the enemy. I will abide in thy tabernacle for ever: I will trust in the covert of thy wings. Selah. Psalms 61:1-4

Here the psalmist ties all these Hebrew words picture together in one glorious portrait of what a relationship with God comprises. In it we see the Lord as a shelter (machaceh – a derivative of chacah) which is the place of His presence we seek; we abide in His tabernacle (ohel – the place of worship); we trust in the covert (cethar – the hiding place), of His wings (kanaph – the sheltered place). This presents an all encompassing tapestry of God's covenant benefits.

Chapter Three

As He so often did, God gave the nation of Israel an everyday-life object lesson to remind them constantly of His promises, protection, and provision. In this case it was what we know today as a 'tallit'. Tallit is an Aramaic word meaning covering. While scripture does not specifically name the tallit, the concept is founded in a commandment contained in Numbers 15:

And the LORD spake unto Moses, saying, Speak unto the children of Israel, and bid them that they make them fringes in the borders of their garments throughout their generations, and that they put upon the fringe of the borders a ribband of blue: And it shall be unto you for a fringe, that ye may look upon it, and remember all the commandments of the LORD, and do them; and that ye seek not after your own heart and your own eyes, after which ye use to go a whoring: That ye may remember, and do all my commandments, and be holy unto your God. Num 15:37-40

The word translated 'garments' here is the Hebrew word 'beged'. The Israelites were instructed to attach fringes: 'tsiytsith' in Hebrew, to their garments as a reminder of His commandments. In fact, the knots on the tsiytsith by rabbinical tradition represent each of the commandments contained in the law of Moses. The idea of a separate and distinct prayer shawl or tallit is a Talmudic development of post-Biblical times. The cloth portion of the tallit is the beged and the fringes are the tsiytsith. This was apparently a measure based strictly on convenience. As people began to accumulate more and more articles of clothing, this tradition was adopted so as not to have to attach fringes to each and every garment one owned. The tallit was worn as a top mantel over all other garments originally, however, in some countries where the Jews were persecuted it began to be worn under the top garment with only the fringes showing in order to avoid drawing unwanted attention from a hostile Gentile populace.

It is vital to understanding the relevance of this passage to realize that the word 'borders' is in fact 'kanaph'. This immediately brings the tallit into the discussion of divine protection. As previously mentioned; the root word of tallit means covering. Deuteronomy 22 gives further instructions on the tallit:

Thou shalt not wear a garment of divers sorts, as of woollen and linen together. Thou shalt make thee fringes upon the four quarters of thy vesture, wherewith thou coverest thyself. Deut 22:11-12

Notice that they were not allowed to make any garments from blended textiles. The use of mixed fiber cloth was reserved for the priests' robes. While this distinction separated the priests as a distinct class, it is also clear that the ordinary citizen was under God's covering as well. With multiple New Testament admonitions that we as believers are 'priests and kings', that separation of classes is done away with. The word 'quarters' once again is 'kanaph'. The connection is obviously not lost on orthodox Jews; who to this day refer to the 'wings' of their tallit. As the Mosaic and Rabbinical traditions developed, we begin to see references to these concepts in Old Testament scripture. The prophet Haggai records the following passage:

Thus saith the LORD of hosts; Ask now the priests concerning the law, saying, If one bear holy flesh in the skirt of his garment, and with his skirt do touch bread, or pottage, or wine, or oil, or any meat, shall it be holy? And the priests answered and said, No. Hag 2:11-12

This scripture is a sort of pop quiz given by God Himself to the priests concerning the handling of sacrifices relative to their garments and ceremonial defilement. It clearly references their outer garment (tallit) and uses the word 'skirt' referring to the extremities of this garment. This word is again the Hebrew word kanaph and introduces the concept of the robe or outer garment representing a covering of righteousness. Zechariah continues in this vein when he pens:

Thus saith the LORD of hosts; In those days it shall come to pass, that ten men shall take hold out of all languages of the nations, even shall take hold of the skirt of him that is a Jew, saying, We will go with you: for we have heard that God is with you. Zech 8:23

This is a prophecy of a time when the Gentile nations, recognizing the Jews' righteous relationship with God and His protective covering of them, will seek to come under that covenant protection by symbolically taking hold of his skirt (kanaph). The skirt or wings of the outer garment became synonymous with the covering and authority of the individual wearing it. The prophet/judge Samuel displayed this in his judgment of King Saul:

And as Samuel turned about to go away, he laid hold upon the skirt of his mantle, and it rent. And Samuel said unto him, The LORD hath rent the kingdom of Israel from thee this day, and hath given it to a neighbour of thine, that is better than thou. 1 Sam 15:27-28

As Psalm 91 portrays, the skirt of the robe, i.e. the kanaph or wings, represented the covering produced by the space underneath. Saul as king of Israel was their spiritual and governmental covering but had that authority and position symbolically torn from him by his rebellion and eventually transferred to King David.

Ezekiel uses this same language to depict God's action in coming into covenant with Israel:

Now when I passed by thee, and looked upon thee, behold, thy time was the time of love; and I spread my skirt over thee, and covered thy nakedness: yea, I sware unto thee, and entered into a covenant with thee, saith the Lord GOD, and thou becamest mine. Ezek 16:8

Once again the word translated skirt is kanaph. The Lord describes Israel as polluted, naked, and destitute and yet in His love He spread His skirt over the nation and 'entered into a covenant with…' them. This shows His covering of protection and authority over them. In chapter two we examined the first encounter between Ruth and Boaz. Now lets look at the final unfolding of this dramatic romance:

And when Boaz had eaten and drunk, and his heart was merry, he went to lie down at the end of the heap of corn: and she came softly, and uncovered his feet, and laid her down. And it came to pass at midnight, that the man was afraid, and turned himself: and, behold, a woman lay at his feet. And he said, Who art thou? And she answered, I am Ruth thine handmaid: spread therefore thy skirt over thine handmaid; for thou art a near kinsman. Ruth 3:7-9

In this narrative is portrayed the exact same description from Ezekiel's passage. Just as the Lord says He covered Israel with His skirt, entering into covenant; Ruth is asking Boaz to do the same and fulfill the covenant requirements of Levirate marriage. She placed herself at his feet in a position of submission and invited him to cover her with his authority and provision.

We see these same themes continue in New Testament writings. Matthew records Jesus' reference to the Jewish garments in the Sermon on the Mount.

And if any man will sue thee at the law, and take away thy coat, let him have thy cloke also. Matt 5:40

This verse is unique in its depiction of the multiple garments worn by the Jews. Here we have first the coat: the Greek 'chiton'; The Hebrew word is 'chaluq'. The Aramaic renders it 'kittuna'. These words refer to the undergarment tunic. The word translated 'cloke' is the Greek 'himation'. This was in the fashion of those days the outermost garment; in the Jews case the tallit. The traditional Jewish dress in the time of Christ consisted of the innermost clothing or Hebrew 'aphqarsin'; what we would call underwear. This was followed by the chiton. Then came then himation or tallit over all. Hence the admonition that a person who took away your tunic should be given your tallit as well.

We see a magnificent, yet tragic outplaying of the stripping of power and authority at the foot of the cross. Jesus already had been deprived of His tallit during His trial as the soldiers mocked Him by putting a purple robe (himation) over Him. This depicts the fact that He had laid aside His authority as God come in the flesh in order to allow Himself to be humiliated in the mockery of a trial He was given. We then see Him at the crucifixion scene being deprived of his inner garment (chaluq) by the Roman soldiers. John 19:23-24 says:

Then the soldiers, when they had crucified Jesus, took his garments, and made four parts, to every soldier a part; and also his coat: now the **coat was without seam, woven from the top throughout**. They said therefore among themselves, Let us not rend it, but cast lots for it, whose it shall be: that the scripture might be fulfilled, which saith, They parted my raiment among them, and for my vesture they did cast lots. These things therefore the soldiers did. John 19:23-24

This is possibly the clearest confirmation of Jesus' status as a rabbi. A rabbi's chaluq was by rabbinical tradition to be close fitting and reach to the feet. It must also be woven seamlessly from top to bottom, just as the passage indicates, indicating why it was considered too valuable to destroy by the soldiers.

In Luke 24:49 Jesus instructs the disciples not to leave Jerusalem until they are 'endued with power from on high'. Only by being filled and empowered by the Holy Spirit can we exercise the authority the tallit represents and it is therefore useless without that power. In the case where our adversary steals our spiritual power (represented by the chaluq) we may as well abandon the pretense of authority and surrender the tallit too! This recalls Saul's fall from authority when his sin and rebellion robbed him of spiritual power. His authority was symbolically stripped by Samuel, but had in fact already departed. David was anointed king almost immediately after Samuel's pronouncement even though Saul was still reigning.

In Matthew 23:5 Jesus chides the Pharisees for their ostentatious enlarging of the tsiytsith of their tallits to make a public show and draw attention to themselves. This was perhaps an attempt at physical, outward compensation for the inward, spiritual bankruptcy they were living in.

But all their works they do for to be seen of men: they make broad their phylacteries, and enlarge the borders of their garments, Matt 23:5

To see further evidence of the New Testament dress let's examine Matthew 9:

And, behold, a woman, which was diseased with an issue of blood twelve years, came behind him, and touched the hem of his garment: For she said within herself, If I may but touch his garment, I shall be whole. Matt 9:20-21

The Greek word rendered 'hem' is 'kraspedon' which is the equivalent of the Hebrew tsiytsith. The word for garment is again himation referring to his tallit. Here the diseased woman reaches out by faith to touch the tsiytsith of Jesus tallit, believing that in those knotted cords she was touching a point of contact to God's covenant promise that he was Jehovah Rapha; 'the Lord that heals you'. Apparently she was correct in this assumption as she was instantly made whole.

Another instance involving healing takes place in Mark 5:

While he yet spake, there came from the ruler of the synagogue's house certain which said, Thy daughter is dead: why troublest thou the Master any further? As soon as Jesus heard the word that was spoken, he saith unto the ruler of the synagogue, Be not afraid, only believe... when he had put them all out, he taketh the father and the mother of the damsel, and them that were with him, and entereth in where the damsel was lying. And he took the damsel by the hand, and said unto her, Talitha cumi; which is, being interpreted, Damsel, I say unto thee, arise. And straightway the damsel arose, and walked... Mark 5:35-43

Here we find the Saviour using an interesting combination of words. He says 'Talitha cumi', an Aramaic phrase meaning 'damsel arise'. Yet hidden within this wording is what many scholars believe is a plays on words; a subtle double entendre; maybe even a pun for the benefit of the select group He allowed to observe the proceedings. Notice the word 'Talitha' and its similarity to the word tallit. It is held by many modern commentators that what He was actually saying was 'young woman under the tallit, arise'; and that He had in fact covered her with His tallit before speaking His resurrecting command. She had died while under her father's covering and authority, but by being placed under Jesus' tallit she was brought under His covering and authority! Death and disease had no answer when brought into subjection to Jesus power and authority.

The final passage I want to look at is found in Matthew chapter 23:

O Jerusalem, Jerusalem, thou that killest the prophets, and stonest them which are sent unto thee, how often would I have gathered thy children together, even as a hen gathereth her chickens under her wings, and ye would not! Behold, your house is left unto you desolate.
Matt 23:37-38

Here we see a depiction of Jesus' love for His chosen people, and yet they refused to come under His protective covering and care. Once again the picture of being gathered under the wings of divine protection is presented as Jesus opens His heart to Jerusalem which would soon be razed to the ground. Under His 'wings' she could have been protected and delivered from Roman oppression and ultimate destruction, but they refused to accept His offered sanctuary.

Chapter Four

In chapter three we examined the tallit, both as an article of clothing, and also its inferences as a covering. We then took those thoughts to their logical conclusion as regards our covering. Jesus himself emphasized the essential nature of this covering when he told the disciples:

And ye are witnesses of these things. And, behold, I send the promise of my Father upon you: but tarry ye in the city of Jerusalem, until ye be endued with power from on high. And he led them out as far as to Bethany, and he lifted up his hands, and blessed them. And it came to pass, while he blessed them, he was parted from them, and carried up into heaven. Luke 24:48-51

He was showing them just how vitally important it was to be endued – literally 'clothed upon' – with the Holy Spirit before they began their ministry. Jesus was no doubt speaking in the rabbinical language and vernacular of his office. The rabbis taught that a man could rescue garments from a burning house on the Sabbath day, but not by carrying them out. He had to put them on, one at a time, and then walk out. He was showing them that they could not carry this burden; they had to be clothed with the anointing of His Spirit and walk out the calling that He had placed on them under that covering! The Greek word here, 'enduo', suggests sinking into a garment. We are to sink, in our own estimation, into His power and glory; and let it cover our fallen humanness so that we can be effective and empowered in pursuing his plans and purposes for our lives. Jesus modeled this for us, as it is recorded in Philippians:

Let this mind be in you, which was also in Christ Jesus: Who, being in the form of God, thought it not robbery to be equal with God: But made himself of no reputation, and took upon him the form of a servant, and was made in the likeness of men: And being found in fashion as a man, he humbled himself, and became obedient unto death, even the death of the cross. Phil 2:6-8

Jesus emptied himself of honor and glory so that we, in due time, could be clothed upon by the same honor and glory he laid aside. This clothing takes an unexpected form when we look at **how and why** we are clothed with glory.

Now we will also look at the process of 'entering in'. After all, the whole point of having a covering (the tallit and garments are symbolic of this covering) is to enter in or move under that covering for protection and refuge from the elements. As previously discussed the entire point of the concept of the booths used at Sukkot, or Feast of Tabernacles, was to provide just such a place of entering in so that the worshipper could have a close, private communion with the Lord. This secret place was entered into and occupied for the duration of the feast days as a place of separation from the normal, day-to-day activities of life. This is precisely the vehicle for the type of communion with God that was intended. Jesus taught His followers to pray in this way:

And when thou prayest, thou shalt not be as the hypocrites are: for they love to pray standing in the synagogues and in the corners of the streets, that they may be seen of men. Verily I say unto you, They have their reward. But thou, when thou prayest, enter into thy closet, and when thou hast shut thy door, pray to thy Father which is in secret; and thy Father which seeth in secret shall reward thee openly. Matt 6:5-6

The Greek word translated secret place here is 'tameion'. It referred to a secret chamber or room. It originally denoted a storeroom or store house, but also came, in time, to take on the latter meaning of room. Matthew 24 and Luke 12 clearly show its interchangeability in these two usages:

Wherefore if they shall say unto you, Behold, he is in the desert; go not forth: behold, he is in the secret chambers; believe it not. Matt 24:26

Here in Matthew it is rendered 'secret chambers'. And…

Therefore whatsoever ye have spoken in darkness shall be heard in the light; and that which ye have spoken in the ear in closets shall be proclaimed upon the housetops. Luke 12:3

Luke gives us the same inference as the Matthew chapter 6 passage: 'closet'. Our 'secret place' is to be a place of solitude in which we minister before God. Just as the high priest always entered the Holy of Holies alone, we must enter into this spiritual holy place alone. We alone can do business of this deeply personal spiritual nature with our heavenly Father. No one can do it for us or with us. True, others can intercede on our behalf; but it is up to each of us individually to conduct those deepest spiritual transactions with the Lord. It is little wonder that Paul exclaims: 'What? know ye not that your body is the temple of the Holy Ghost which is in you…' 1 Cor 6:19. (more on this in chapter seven!)

Entering the secret place brings us into the manifest presence of our Father. Nowhere could there possibly be a safer place of refuge. Psalm 16 records these phrases:

Thou wilt shew me the path of life: **in thy presence** is fulness of joy; **at thy right hand** there are pleasures for evermore. Psalms 16:11 (emphasis mine)

If we are to enter into His presence in the manner of a priest, first of all **we have to have a High Priest to follow**, next **we have to be made priests,** and finally **we have to be clothed in priests' garments.**

Wherein God, willing more abundantly to shew unto the heirs of promise the immutability of his counsel, confirmed it by an oath: That by two immutable things, in which it was impossible for God to lie, we might have a strong consolation, who have fled for refuge to lay hold upon the hope set before us: Which hope we have as an anchor of the soul, both sure and stedfast, and which entereth into that within the veil; **Whither the forerunner is for us entered, even Jesus, made an high priest for ever after the order of Melchisedec.** Heb 6:18-20 (emphasis mine)

Here we have the first part of the requirements covered: Jesus was the great high priest of our faith. He established a better priesthood that that of Aaron under the Old Testament law. He also opened the way for us to be established as priests of this new order. John penned the following words in the book of Revelation:

And they sung a new song, saying, Thou art worthy to take the book, and to open the seals thereof: for thou wast slain, and hast redeemed us to God by thy blood out of every kindred, and tongue, and people, and nation; And hast made us unto our God kings and priests: and we shall reign on the earth. Rev 5:9-10

Lastly, as we have already seen in Luke 24, we have been clothed by the Holy Spirit in the necessary priests' garments to carry out the ministry he has set forth for us. Notice also that Hebrews 6 describes this place of priestly ministry in these terms: 'That... we might have a strong consolation, who have fled for refuge'. Even under the Old Testament regime it was believed that the temple and its precincts were a place of refuge and divine protection. It is a tragic twist of this belief that when the Roman

Tenth Legion invaded the city of Jerusalem in 70 A.D. the Jewish people fled into the temple compound in the sincere, but misguided, belief that God would supernaturally protect them there. Sadly, they failed to understand that the physical temple was not the true 'secret place'. It was an earthly shadow of the heavenly. If they had sought the spiritual rather than cling to the physical they may have been spared. History tells us that hundreds of thousands died in the flames as Roman soldiers torched the city. On the other hand, believers in Christ, having been warned prophetically, fled Jerusalem months in advance and none were killed in the massacre. Those believers abandoned Jerusalem and the physical temple, but they carried their true 'secret place' with them in the form of their faith-filled relationship with God. Even though they were refugees in the earth, in the heavenlies they were sheltered under his wings as they trusted in and acted on His prophetic guidance.

Chapter Five

It is impossible to fully comprehend the complexities of the meaning and symbolism behind the tallit without understanding its historical usages and the tie-ins to many other areas of symbolic and prophetic significance in scripture. Historically one of the first external uses of the tallit was as the wedding canopy. In early times, what we know as the chuppah or wedding canopy was simply a tallit draped over the couples' shoulders, both at the betrothal, and at the actual marriage ceremony. This represented their covering in covenant with God and is a very apropos word picture for our study. Once again we see the concept of being covered beneath His wings – the wings or corners of the tallit – as a picture of God's shelter and protection. Later the tallit was draped over a canopy framework as the custom evolved toward our modern chuppah. This was a gradual process as the roles and purpose of the canopy began to take on additional significance.

It is vital to know, however, that simultaneously there was another tradition that was evolving: the wedding chamber. This was a room or enclosure that was the place of the consummation of the marriage. This chamber could be a room or chamber in the groom's parents' dwelling, or it could be a free-standing structure. (more on this later) The earliest uses of the word chuppah are found in Old Testament scripture. David is the first to use the word in Psalm 19:

Which is as a bridegroom coming out of his chamber, and rejoiceth as a strong man to run a race. Psalms 19:5

Here he refers to chuppah in the original meaning of the Hebrew word as the wedding chamber. The prophet Joel uses a combination of Hebrew words that give us further insight into the nuances of meaning for chuppah. Joel says in chapter 2:

Gather the people, sanctify the congregation, assemble the elders… let the bridegroom go forth of his chamber, and the bride out of her closet. Joel 2:16

The word translated 'closet' is chuppah. The word translated chamber here is 'cheder', which means literally, innermost place. This verse represents a type of Hebraism, or Jewish figure of speech, in which the same thing is said twice in two different ways to add emphasis to what is being spoken. It is noteworthy that even in this somewhat artificial construction the words are chosen extremely carefully to convey a subtle extra meaning. While cheder means innermost place or part, chuppah comes from the root 'chaphah' which means to cover. It seems the whole of our narrative is interlaced with these shades of connotation referring to God's covering in the secret place.

According to the Babylonian Talmud, when a boy or girl was born a cedar tree was planted. When a couple was married their trees were cut down and the branches were woven together to create their chuppah – their innermost intimate place. How so like the symbolism we previously discussed for the Sukkot – our innermost chamber to commune with God in intimacy! Eventually people's sensibilities of privacy created a societal atmosphere in which the two traditions: the chuppah and the wedding canopy, were melded into one. The couple was married under the chuppah in public and then traveled to the groom's father's dwelling for the joining together as one.

This practice reveals a symbolic picture that shows us how the relationship between a husband and wife in covenant to each other, and to God, fits together. This representation of the bride and groom in relation to the covering becomes even more compelling when we remember that Israel is described as God's wife. Jeremiah penned these words:

They say, If a man put away his wife, and she go from him, and become another man's, shall he return unto her again? shall not that land be greatly polluted? but thou hast played the harlot with many lovers; yet return again to me, saith the LORD... Surely as a wife treacherously departeth from her husband, so have ye dealt treacherously with me, O house of Israel, saith the LORD. Jer 3:1;20

In this passage is a depiction of the interaction of an unfaithful wife – Israel and a longsuffering husband – God. But notice that in the entirety of Old Testament scripture never does God break his half of the covenant. In fact when the Lord made his covenant with Abraham (a forerunner of Abraham's descendants, i.e. Israel) he did all the 'covenanting':

And he said unto him, I am the LORD that brought thee out of Ur of the Chaldees, to give thee this land to inherit it. And he said, Lord GOD, whereby shall I know that I shall inherit it? And he said unto him, Take me an heifer of three years old, and a she goat of three years old, and a ram of three years old, and a turtledove, and a young pigeon. And he took unto him all these, and divided them in the midst, and laid each piece one against another: but the birds divided he not. And when the fowls came down upon the carcases, Abram drove them away. And when the sun was going down, a deep sleep fell upon Abram; and, lo, an horror of great darkness fell upon him. And he said unto Abram, Know of a surety that thy seed shall be a stranger in a land that is not theirs, and shall serve them; and they shall afflict them four hundred years; And also that nation, whom they shall serve, will I judge: and afterward shall they come out with great substance. And thou shalt go to thy fathers in peace; thou shalt be buried in a good old age. But in the fourth generation they shall come hither again: for the iniquity of the Amorites is not yet full. And it came to pass, that, when the sun went down, and it was dark, behold a smoking furnace, and a burning lamp that passed between those pieces. In the same day the LORD made a covenant with Abram, saying, Unto thy seed have I given this land, from the river of Egypt unto the great river, the river Euphrates... Gen 15:7-18

Abraham was in 'a deep sleep' so that the covenant ritual, which required both parties to walk through the animal sacrifices while reciting the vows of the covenant, was carried out completely by God. The Lord left nothing to chance as he permitted no avenue for human weakness and frailty to wreck what he was putting into motion. Just as God would allow no breach in his physical, earthly covenant with Israel, there was not an option for the spiritual marriage covenant between himself and his wife. In the same way that an earthly husband and wife were covered during the wedding ceremony by the symbol of God's covenant – a tallit – the Lord is described in Psalm 91 as having us covered under his wings.

Chapter Six

In chapter five we examined the scriptural concept of Israel being portrayed as God's wife. Simultaneous to this symbolic theme's development there is another prophetic picture that begins to emerge: the bride that is being chosen and raised up for God's own Son! This is the greatest surprise of all the scriptures: how God himself planned to create and raise up a Gentile bride that was specifically chosen for Jesus. Paul says in Romans 11:

For I would not, brethren, that ye should be ignorant of this mystery, lest ye should be wise in your own conceits; that blindness in part is happened to Israel, until the fulness of the Gentiles be come in. Romans 11:25

Notice that Paul calls the idea of God taking a Gentile people to himself a mystery. This seems counterintuitive considering God's almost universally negative posture toward Gentiles in the Old Testament. However, he gave us a tiny encoded hint into his intentions in the Genesis account of the selection of Isaac's bride Rebekkah. This story is a prophetic picture of Christ and his bride. In Genesis 24 Abraham tells his servant:

And Abraham was old, and well stricken in age: and the LORD had blessed Abraham in all things. And Abraham said unto his eldest servant of his house, that ruled over all that he had, Put, I pray thee, thy hand under my thigh: And I will make thee swear by the LORD, the God of heaven, and the God of the earth, that thou shalt not take a wife unto my son of the daughters of the Canaanites, among whom I dwell: But thou shalt go unto my country, and to my kindred, and take a wife unto my son Isaac. Gen 24:1-4

Here we see Abraham specifically instructing his servant to go into Abraham's native country to choose a bride for Isaac. Why is this important symbolically? Because Abraham was a Gentile! Here we see the father of the Jewish nation, the patriarch of all patriarchs, acquiring a Gentile bride for his own son. This is a clearly a picture of what God was going to do with His son, just as surely as Abraham's sacrifice of Isaac on Mount Moriah was a prophetic picture of how God would sacrifice his son for us.

In the New Testament we begin to catch glimpses of this idea as early as John the Baptist's ministry. St. John pens these words in his gospel:

Ye yourselves bear me witness, that I said, I am not the Christ, but that I am sent before him. He that hath the bride is the bridegroom: but the friend of the bridegroom, which standeth and heareth him, rejoiceth greatly because of the bridegroom's voice: this my joy therefore is fulfilled. He must increase, but I must decrease. John 3:28-30

This is the first New Testament reference to the concept of the bridegroom and his bride. John the Baptist clearly identifies himself as the 'friend of the bridegroom' and Christ as the bridegroom. There is no indication of who the bride is at this point – it is doubtful if John himself understood what he said prophetically – but, we know from this point forward that she definitely exists. St. John had the privilege of introducing the bride, and he was the one chosen by God to see her by prophetic revelation in the Apocalypse.

And there came unto me one of the seven angels which had the seven vials full of the seven last plagues, and talked with me, saying, Come hither, I will shew thee the bride, the Lamb's wife. Rev 21:9

Jesus himself elaborated on this theme when he said (also penned by St. John):

In my Father's house are many mansions: if it were not so, I would have told you. I go to prepare a place for you. And if I go and prepare a place for you, I will come again, and receive you unto myself; that where I am, there ye may be also. John 14:2-3

This passage seems pedestrian enough until one realizes that this language is taken directly from the Jewish betrothal and wedding traditions. Notice that he says there are many 'mansions', or in Greek, mone which are dwelling places. This is the reason this passage is so important. He is bringing the Old Testament idea of covering and shelter into the new covenant. In the first part of the Olivet Discourse in Matthew 23-25, Jesus reinforces the covenant promise of covering.

O Jerusalem, Jerusalem, thou that killest the prophets, and stonest them which are sent unto thee, how often would I have gathered thy children together, even as a hen gathereth her chickens under her wings, and ye would not! Matt 23:37

This is directly reminiscent of the Psalm 91 reference to the shelter under God's wings. This notion takes on a whole new level of significance when we remember that the Jewish betrothal and wedding ceremonies both occurred beneath the shelter of the overspread tallit. This idea is seen as far back as the story of Ruth and Boaz. When Ruth seeks to have Boaz play the role of gaol or kinsman-redeemer she goes to him (at her mother-in-law Naomi's instruction) and lies down at Boaz' feet and asks him to cover her with the skirts – kanaph – of his robe indicating that she was under his authority, care, and protection!

Now that we have a clear understanding of the status of Israel's place as God's wife, and the church's role as the bride of Christ we can begin to properly sort out some of the New Testament scriptures relating to the wedding, the bridegroom, the bride, and the other parties that we are told will attend the ceremony. We have already identified the gentile church as the bride, but what of the others? We examined the Olivet Discourse earlier in regard to the covering of protection. In the latter portion of the same teaching Jesus gives us what is known as the 'parable of the ten virgins'.

Then shall the kingdom of heaven be likened unto ten virgins, which took their lamps, and went forth to meet the bridegroom. And five of them were wise, and five were foolish. They that were foolish took their lamps, and took no oil with them: But the wise took oil in their vessels with their lamps. While the bridegroom tarried, they all slumbered and slept. And at midnight there was a cry made, Behold, the bridegroom cometh; go ye out to meet him. Then all those virgins arose, and trimmed their lamps. And the foolish said unto the wise, Give us of your oil; for our lamps are gone out. But the wise answered, saying, Not so; lest there be not enough for us and you: but go ye rather to them that sell, and buy for yourselves. And while they went to buy, the bridegroom came; and they that were ready went in with him to the marriage: and the door was shut. Afterward came also the other virgins, saying, Lord, Lord, open to us. But he answered and said, Verily I say unto you, I know you not. Watch therefore, for ye know neither the day nor the hour wherein the Son of man cometh. Matt 25:2-13

This has been a grossly misunderstood scripture passage. This has led to a misinterpretation of this parable for centuries by well meaning teachers, preachers and scholars who have tried to force a 'square peg'; the church, into the 'round hole'; i.e. the framework of these verses. – it just plain doesn't work. Why? Because the church is the bride, not the ten virgins. In this parable we see a mystery begin to unfold. Jesus is at the end of his earthly ministry and is answering his disciples' questions about the end of the world; or the end of the age as some translate it. In chapters 24 and 25 he gives his followers a final series of parables; all relating to his second coming and final judgment. Notice that these are kingdom parables and are thus related to the Jews, not the church or the Gentiles. In fact, this parable from the Olivet Discourse is for all practical purposes a commentary on his previous teachings on the bridegroom and bride from the John chapter 14 passage we looked at briefly above. Here he gives us a contrast between the description of the bride in John and the ten virgins in this passage. Notice that John 14 is centered solely on the bridegroom and his bride; and yet, in Matthew 25 there is **no mention** of the bride whatsoever. The coming of the bridegroom is mentioned but not the bride. These verses give us insight into the relationships surrounding the bridegroom, but in some ways only serve to deepen the mystery of the bride vis-à-vis the ten virgins. This has led to all sorts of spurious doctrines and ideas regarding the relationship of Christ to his brethren the Jews and his followers.

The first and key point to this revelation is the understanding that the 'ten virgins' as Jesus calls them ARE NOT Gentile Christians and they ARE NOT the church. This more than anything I can relate here is totally essential to our ability to put this teaching in proper context so that we can fit all the pieces of this theological puzzle together. As I describe the Jewish wedding traditions and how they relate to this parable in the following chapters, these puzzle pieces will hopefully begin to fall into place. In verses two through four of our parable, we begin to see a division or differentiation within the ten virgins:

And five of them were wise, and five were foolish. They that were foolish took their lamps, and took no oil with them: But the wise took oil in their vessels with their lamps. Matt 25:3-4

We see that five are described as wise and five as foolish. Half have oil in their lamps and half have none. Building on the premise that the church is the bride, we would say that this cannot possibly apply to the church, as no one would be so cynical as to say that half of the church was unsaved. Some would have us to believe that the five foolish were those who had been saved and had backslidden into reprobation and ultimate destruction in hell. Again we must look closely at the premise of the parable and the Jewish wedding ceremony. Specifically the coming of the bridegroom for his espoused bride. This process, and it is a process, is something that every person in Israel would have been closely acquainted with.

After all, every married or engaged person had experienced at least part of this. The ten virgins are central to the understanding of Jesus' meaning in this teaching. In the Jewish wedding tradition every young woman who was engaged, or 'espoused' as the scripture puts it, had ten young women - virgins, who were her attendants. There is little doubt that this tradition is the origin of our present day notion of bridesmaids. These ten young women had as their sole responsibility the task of insuring that the bride would be ready for that middle-of-the-night summons by her intended, to come out to him and return to his home for the wedding festivities.

After the betrothal ceremony, which would take place at or near the brides home, the bridegroom would leave the bride behind and return to his home or village. Here he would build a home, or at least a room onto his father's home, for the bride and himself. (in my Father's house are many mansions) When **his father** determined that all was in readiness he would then gather his friends and start the journey to his brides home or village. This trip was timed in such a way as to place his arrival at or near midnight. As the party approached her home a trumpet would be blown and a shout raised: 'behold the bridegroom comes, make ready to meet him.' At this point all unmarried women (this would traditionally take place on Tuesday night for virgins and on Wednesday night for widows or divorced women) would arise with their attendants and ready themselves to go see which young woman's groom was approaching. The united party would then return to his village/home and the wedding would be consummated.

This logically leads us to the 'marriage supper of the lamb' as described in Revelation chapter 19. But what of those mysterious ten virgins? We must understand **all** the parties involved in the 'process'. First we have the 'friends of the bridegroom' who come with him as seen in John 14. Notice that they are where he is prior to the journey and come with him. Symbolically they represent the Old Testament saints who are in heaven and return with him at the rapture. Once again, we have already seen that the bride is the church. There then only remains one group unaccounted for: the Jewish nation. We see the ten virgins **at the bride's dwelling**. These are people who are living on the earth during the time of the bridegroom's absence (i.e. the 'church age'). Notice that half go with him in the rapture and half are left. This clearly points to the fact that part of the Jews will be saved and go in the rapture and part will be left in unbelief to endure the tribulation. These Jews that are taken in the rapture are the 'wedding guests' as described in Matthew chapter 22. Many of the ones invited would not come (the unbelieving Jews) and the wayward strangers (the Gentiles) were invited in their place.

The kingdom of heaven is like unto a certain king, which made a marriage for his son, And sent forth his servants to call them that were bidden to the wedding: and they would not come. Again, he sent forth other servants, saying, Tell them which are bidden, Behold, I have prepared my dinner: my oxen and my fatlings are killed, and all things are ready: come unto the marriage. But they made light of it, and went their ways, one to his farm, another to his merchandise: And the remnant took his servants, and entreated them spitefully, and slew them. But when the king heard thereof, he was wroth: and he sent forth his armies, and destroyed those murderers, and burned up their city. Then saith he to his servants, The wedding is ready, but they which were bidden were not worthy. Go ye therefore into the highways, and as many as ye shall find, bid to the marriage. So those servants went out into the highways, and gathered together all as many as they found, both bad and good: and the wedding was furnished with guests. Matt 22:3-10

This passage shows how absolutely essential it is to be in right relationship with God, i.e. to be properly covered! Luke 12 also shows us a glimpse of the need for readiness:

Let your loins be girded about, and your lights burning; And ye yourselves like unto men that wait for their lord, when he will return from the wedding; that when he cometh and knocketh, they may open unto him immediately. Blessed are those servants, whom the lord when he cometh shall find watching: verily I say unto you, that he shall gird himself, and make them to sit down to meat, and will come forth and serve them. Luke 12:34-37

These verses show us that we all, Jew or gentile, must be prepared to meet him regardless of the time or circumstance.

80

Chapter Seven

Psalm 27 verse five gives us an interesting insight into the 'secret place'.

For in the time of trouble he shall hide me in his pavilion: in the secret of his tabernacle shall he hide me; he shall set me up upon a rock. Psalms 27:5

The second word translated 'hide' is cether – the secret place or hiding place. It has a connotation indicating the innermost chamber or room; a personal dwelling place. This witnesses with our previous word studies on the secret place as a location reserved for private, intimate fellowship with the Lord. In Old Testament times this word would have been used to describe the Holy of Holies; the innermost chamber of the temple. In that spiritual economy only the high priest would have entered that chamber, and that only once a year at the feast of Yom Kippur or Atonement. It was here in the Holy of Holies that God himself met with the high priest in the form of the Shekinah glory of his manifest presence. Surely this is a picture of what the Lord intends for us as we meet with him in the secret place.

The Psalmist pens these words in Psalm 27:

One thing have I desired of the LORD, that will I seek after; that I may dwell in the house of the LORD all the days of my life, to behold the beauty of the LORD, and to enquire in his temple. Psalms 27:4

We should note that the word rendered 'temple' is the Hebrew word heykel, which can mean both temple and palace. As we move farther into this study we will begin to see the parallels between the earthly temple and the heavenly palace/temple. The throne of God is depicted as being located in the heavenly temple. The following excerpts from Bring in the Glory will illustrate:

And the seventh angel poured out his vial into the air; and there came a great voice out of the temple of heaven, from the throne, saying, It is done. Rev 16:17

Notice that the voice is identified as coming both "out of the temple" and "from the throne", positioning the throne firmly in the temple. The Greek word 'apo' is translated both 'out' and 'from' in this verse. This word has a base meaning of movement away from a place or position toward another place or position. This clearly indicates that the throne of God is located within the temple.

The LORD is in his holy temple, the LORD'S throne is in heaven: his eyes behold, his eyelids try, the children of men. Ps 11:4

If God is in his temple and on his throne, then this leaves no doubt as to where God's throne is located and also gives us insight into the dynamics of heavenly worship and the position of God enthroned in his glory. This is vitally important in recognizing the deeper meaning of the descriptions of the heavenly temple found in the New Testament. These are seen as revelatory reflections in the Old Testament tabernacle and temple patterns.

Paul gives us a view into the heavenly worship experience when he penned these words in Hebrews 10:

Having therefore, brethren, boldness to enter into the holiest by the blood of Jesus, By a new and living way, which he hath consecrated for us, through the veil, that is to say, his flesh; Heb 10:20

…when the earthly priest offered the blood of atonement on the earthly mercy seat, he produced a temporary atonement for man that connected with that contact point. Unfortunately that was as far as it reached. However, when Jesus offered his blood on the heavenly mercy seat, he produced a heavenly, eternal atonement that opened the way for heaven to reach into the very hearts of mankind! Now we get a far deeper understanding of the passage:

What? know ye not that your body is the temple of the Holy Ghost which is in you… 1 Corinthians 6:19

The point of contact between the heavenly realm and the earthly; between God and man, has radically changed. No longer is the connection residing above a physical location in a physical temple; it is residing in the believer himself in the person of the Holy Spirit!

John gives us a hint at the true nature of our relationship with the Father when he says:

Behold, what manner of love the Father hath bestowed upon us, that we should be called the sons of God: therefore the world knoweth us not, because it knew him not. Beloved, now are we the sons of God, and it doth not yet appear what we shall be: but we know that, when he shall appear, we shall be like him; for we shall see him as he is. 1 John 3:1-2

John refers to our spiritual adoption as sons of God, but he goes on to point out that while we are not all we should be, we also are not all **we will be**. He brings the passage to its climax with the revelation that when Christ comes we will be like Him! Just as He spent 'quality time' with His Father, we should be spending time in the secret place cultivating our relationship and preparing for the time when we will be in his personal presence just as Christ now is bodily, and we are now spiritually. In fact, Revelation chapter 3 shows us a picture of God's love as being so intense that he won't let the 'overcomers' even leave his presence:

Him that overcometh will I make a pillar in the temple of my God, and **he shall go no more out**: and I will write upon him the name of my God, and the name of the city of my God, which is new Jerusalem, which cometh down out of heaven from my God: and I will write upon him my new name. Rev 3:12 (emphasis mine)

Now notice the logical progression we are presented by Paul in the letter to the Ephesians. First Christ's exaltation is described:

Wherefore I also... Cease not to give thanks for you, making mention of you in my prayers... that ye may know what is the hope of his calling, and what the riches of the glory of his inheritance in the saints, And what is the exceeding greatness of his power to us-ward who believe, according to the working of his mighty power, Which he wrought in Christ, when he raised him from the dead, and set him at his own right hand in the heavenly places, Far above all principality, and power, and might, and dominion, and every name that is named, not only in this world, but also in that which is to come: And hath put all things under his feet, and gave him to be the head over all things to the church, Which is his body, the fulness of him that filleth all in all. Eph 1:15-23

Christ is the head over the church and is seated in 'heavenly places', i.e. in God's throne - 'at his own right hand'. Then Paul goes on to say the we are seated in 'heavenly places':

But God, who is rich in mercy, for his great love wherewith he loved us, Even when we were dead in sins, hath quickened us together with Christ, (by grace ye are saved;) And hath raised us up together, and made us sit together in heavenly places in Christ Jesus: Eph 2:4-6

If, as we have shown, the throne room of God in heaven is actually the Holy of Holies in the heavenly temple, and if we are presently raised up and seated there spiritually, then it stands to reason that we are expected to currently, presently be worshipping and communing with God in what he calls 'the secret place' or his innermost dwelling place or chamber!

In earlier chapters we have seen that the tallit was a covering that symbolized this secret place. What few realize is that in earliest times the bride's veil was considered sufficient as the covering for the wedding ceremony. Just as Hebrews 10 portrays Christ's body as a veil to be penetrated to reach his ultimate destiny at the Father's right hand, we too are separated from the fulness of God's presence by our fleshly bodies. This partition will be done away with at the resurrection and what is now only a spiritual relationship and fellowship will then be face-to-face as 1 Corinthians 13 puts it:

For now we see through a glass, darkly; but then face to face: now I know in part; but then shall I know even as also I am known. 1 Corinthians 13:12

This description becomes even more moving when we realize that Paul, a rabbi in his own right brought up at the feet of Gamaliel as scripture tells us, was writing under the inspiration of the Holy Spirit but also from his own rabbinical background. The rabbis believed and taught that not only are we shielded from God's glory by our flesh, but that God himself also had a covering called in Hebrew the 'pardog', which means a cloudy veil. This glory covering, which can be identified with such earthly manifestations as the Shekinah glory and the pillar of cloud, is a form of celestial, heavenly tallit which covers the Almighty on his throne. The rabbis also taught that only the archangels were permitted inside this covering; the other angelic beings only heard his voice coming from the pardog. How much clearer can this lesson be: if we are to commune with God on the deepest level, we must be in relationship on the deepest level.

Revelation chapter 8 describes an angel offering incense on a golden altar just before God's throne. As we have established God's throne is the true heavenly Holy of Holies, and God is wrapped in his veil of glory which separates him from all but the archangels, then this event is an exact match to the earthly priests offering incense on the altar of incense before the high priest enters the Holy of Holies. Once again the pattern is revealed that worship is the requisite ingredient for preparation to enter the secret place.

Chapter Eight

He that dwelleth in the secret place of the most High shall abide under the shadow of the Almighty. Psalms 91:1

The introduction looks into the Hebrew words translated 'dwelleth' - yashab, and 'abide' – luwn. Once again, yashab has an underlying inference of permanence, while luwn tends to indicate a temporary place of abode. There is another Old Testament word used to describe these concepts. It is found in psalm 61 rendered as 'abide':

From the end of the earth will I cry unto thee, when my heart is overwhelmed: lead me to the rock that is higher than I. For thou hast been a shelter for me, and a strong tower from the enemy. I will abide in thy tabernacle for ever: I will trust in the covert of thy wings. Psalms 61:2-4

Here the Hebrew word is 'guwr', which means to sojourn or dwell in a place that is not native to you, as a visitor. It is interesting that this particular word is only used as a verb in Hebrew, and is only found as a noun in the other northern Semitic languages and dialects. Presumably this is because the other nations and tribes of that area were more or less permanent in their dwellings and used the word to describe an extended trip or journey; whereas the people of Israel had a long history of being nomadic sojourners in lands where they were strangers.

This speaks to us as New Testament believers, first of the idea of our living in this world in which we are physically natives, but spiritually we are sojourners whose citizenship is in the heavenlies. Secondly, and more important for this treatise, it speaks to the fact that when we enter the secret place we are visitors to a realm spiritually that we are not native occupants of physically. The veil of our flesh prevents us from the fulness of our relationship and fellowship with God and Christ.

The New Testament scriptures have much to say on this subject also. John used the Greek word 'meno' to describe this concept. In fact, of the 120 times this Greek verb is used in the New testament, nearly half of them are in John's writings. He used this word in meanings that are rendered: abide, remain, continue, endure, and tarry. The Strong's Exhaustive Concordance tells us it means 'to stay in a given place, state, relation, or expectancy'. Notice the words 'relation' and 'expectancy'. This is just the concept we are studying; the relationship with, and expectancy of encounter with, the Almighty as we enter into and abide in that secret place! Small wonder John used this word over and over to convey his message of abiding in Christ to the 1st century disciples. In chapter one of his Gospel, John uses meno to denote an ordinary, earthly dwelling:

Again the next day after John stood, and two of his disciples; And looking upon Jesus as he walked, he saith, Behold the Lamb of God! And the two disciples heard him speak, and they followed Jesus. Then Jesus turned, and saw them following, and saith unto them, What seek ye? They said unto him, Rabbi, (which is to say, being interpreted, Master,) where dwellest thou? He saith unto them, Come and see. They came and saw where he dwelt, and abode with him that day: for it was about the tenth hour. John 1:35-39

Notice that just as in the Hebrew, the Greek use of 'abode' is a verb. Abiding in the secret place is an activity, not just a geographic position or physical posture. Jesus quoted Isaiah 29 when he said: "well did Esaias prophesy of you, saying, This people draweth nigh unto me with their mouth, and honoureth me with their lips; but their heart is far from me." As the earlier chapters of this writing make clear, entering in to the secret place involves worship, fellowship, and personal communion with God. It is not merely going into a specific room, chamber, or other location, it is an encounter. Jesus made this clear to the apostle Phillip when he gently rebuked him for not understanding the principle of relationship with the Father through the Son:

Philip saith unto him, Lord, shew us the Father, and it sufficeth us. Jesus saith unto him, Have I been so long time with you, and yet hast thou not known me, Philip? he that hath seen me hath seen the Father; and how sayest thou then, Shew us the Father? Believest thou not that I am in the Father, and the Father in me? the words that I speak unto you I speak not of myself: but the Father that dwelleth in me, he doeth the works. Believe me that I am in the Father, and the Father in me: or else believe me for the very works' sake. Verily, verily, I say unto you, He that believeth on me, the works that I do shall he do also; and greater works than these shall he do; because I go unto my Father. And whatsoever ye shall ask in my name, that will I do, that the Father may be glorified in the Son. If ye shall ask any thing in my name, I will do it. If ye love me, keep my commandments. And I will pray the Father, and he shall give you another Comforter, that he may abide with you for ever; Even the Spirit of truth; whom the world cannot receive, because it seeth him not, neither knoweth him: but ye know him; for he dwelleth with you, and shall be in you. John 14:8-17

Here again we see the words 'dwell' and 'abide' used repeatedly, underscoring the essential nature of the intimate intertwining of God and man that their interaction would produce. This was the divine will and purpose for God's ultimate creation from the foundation of the world. Even in Eden this reaching out to man by the Lord was evident:

And the LORD God formed man of the dust of the ground, and breathed into his nostrils the breath of life; and man became a living soul. And the LORD God planted a garden eastward in Eden; and there he put the man whom he had formed. And out of the ground made the LORD God to grow every tree that is pleasant to the sight, and good for food; the tree of life also in the midst of the garden, and the tree of knowledge of good and evil… And they heard the voice of the LORD God walking in the garden in the cool of the day: and Adam and his wife hid themselves from the presence of the LORD God amongst the trees of the garden. Gen 2:7-9; 3:8

God had from the very beginning sought a people to be in perfect fellowship and relationship with, but the fall interrupted his plan – notice the word interrupted. It was reconciled and brought back into order by Christ on the cross. This is what Jesus was attempting to teach the twelve in his discourse in John 15:

I am the true vine, and my Father is the husbandman. Every branch in me that beareth not fruit he taketh away: and every branch that beareth fruit, he purgeth it, that it may bring forth more fruit. Now ye are clean through the word which I have spoken unto you. Abide in me, and I in you. As the branch cannot bear fruit of itself, except it abide in the vine; no more can ye, except ye abide in me. I am the vine, ye are the branches: He that abideth in me, and I in him, the same bringeth forth much fruit: for without me ye can do nothing. If a man abide not in me, he is cast forth as a branch, and is withered; and men gather them, and cast them into the fire, and they are burned. If ye abide in me, and my words abide in you, ye shall ask what ye will, and it shall be done unto you. John 15:1-7

Jesus' words make it abundantly clear that the relationship won't always be easy or comfortable, but it will be for the ultimate good of the believer. Words like 'purge' and 'lift up' sound daunting, but the love of the Father will overcome all. By the same token, he presents a picture of the total interdependency of the fellowship of the Father, the Son, the Holy Spirit, and we ourselves as believers:

Beloved, if God so loved us, we ought also to love one another. No man hath seen God at any time. If we love one another, God dwelleth in us, and his love is perfected in us. Hereby know we that we dwell in him, and he in us, because he hath given us of his Spirit. And we have seen and do testify that the Father sent the Son to be the Saviour of the world. Whosoever shall confess that Jesus is the Son of God, God dwelleth in him, and he in God. And we have known and believed the love that God hath to us. God is love; and he that dwelleth in love dwelleth in God, and God in him. 1 John 4:11-16

In this brief passage the word 'dwell' and its variants are used no less than five times! It is stated that our relationship with our Christian brothers and sisters, our confession before the world, and our spirituality are direct indicators of the level of our dwelling or abiding in him. Only in the secret place can we be transformed from the carnal, fallen creatures we all naturally tend to be, into the love-filled spiritual beings he intend us to be.

Chapter Nine

The Lord has very openly demonstrated his intentions regarding creation in general and mankind specifically, from the very foundation of the world. It has been said by theologians from time past memory: "if you want to see God's plan for man, just look at the first two chapters of Genesis and the last two chapters of Revelation". What you will see is God and man (along with the rest of creation) in perfect harmony and relationship. As chapter 8 points out, in Genesis, God creates a garden and places man there. It is obvious from the ensuing passages that it was his intention to have fellowship with man there. Sin broke that fellowship for long ages. There intervenes many centuries filled with the tension created by man's attempt to create a relationship with God by his own efforts, conflicting with God's attempt to restore man to fellowship in accordance with his eternal plan and purpose. In Revelation chapter three we get a glimpse into the playing out of these plans and purposes:

To him that overcometh will I grant to sit with me in my throne, even as I also overcame, and am set down with my Father in his throne. Rev 3:21

This verse, which we have already examined, show man in an exalted state with the worship of God as the central focus of his existence. Verse 22 goes on to say that these glorified humans will 'no longer go out': God won't even allow them to leave his presence.

In those intervening years and centuries, however, there were scriptural hints, veiled prophesies, and religious ceremonies that weren't comprehended by the people as to their meaning and purpose. They can now, from our historic viewpoint, be pieced together, layer upon layer to produce a wonderful tapestry of God's will displayed for us to see. The scriptures regarding marriage, specifically God's 'marriage' to Israel, coupled with the traditions surrounding the chuppah or wedding canopy begin to meld together in a comprehensive picture when viewed through the lens of Jesus' teaching on the Second Coming, marriage, the parable of the ten virgins, etc. When we remember that the original chuppahs were merely a tallit stretched over a simple canopy frame, there begins to emerge another connection of great significance. The Tabernacle of David was in reality a large, economy-sized chuppah. It wasn't a tent or tabernacle in the normal sense of the word in that it was open on the sides for all to see the ark it was covering.

One can draw a line of symbolic meaning and spiritual purpose directly from those earliest tallit-style chuppahs, to the Tabernacle of David, to the words of Psalm 27 and Psalm 91, to the booths constructed in the celebration of Sukkot or Tabernacles, to Jesus' teaching on entering the closet to pray. There is a continuous thread of understanding concerning an enclosed place for man to commune with his creator. Even in those spiritually troubled ages God was reaching out for a fellowship experience with the pinnacle of his creation.

Even though all mankind was awed by the glory of Solomon's Temple, there was something sacred and special about those secret place encounters. We see this played out in David's life. In approximately 1042 BC, David retrieves the ark from the house of Obed and brings the ark into the city of Jerusalem. He then erects the tabernacle for it to rest under:

And it was told king David, saying, The LORD hath blessed the house of Obededom, and all that pertaineth unto him, because of the ark of God. So David went and brought up the ark of God from the house of Obededom into the city of David with gladness. And it was so, that when they that bare the ark of the LORD had gone six paces, he sacrificed oxen and fatlings. And David danced before the LORD with all his might; and David was girded with a linen ephod. So David and all the house of Israel brought up the ark of the LORD with shouting, and with the sound of the trumpet. And as the ark of the LORD came into the city of David, Michal Saul's daughter looked through a window, and saw king David leaping and dancing before the LORD; and she despised him in her heart. And they brought in the ark of the LORD, and set it in his place, in the midst of **the tabernacle that David had pitched for it**: and David offered burnt offerings and peace offerings before the LORD. 2 Sam 6:12-17 (emphasis mine)

Here the Hebrew word translated tabernacle is 'ohel' which simply means a tent. At this point it is merely a place to house the ark. Notice that as David's relationship with the Lord matures the role and purpose of that tent changes. By 1034 BC, following the Bathsheba incident, when David is going to pray before the ark to ask God's mercy for his son, the tabernacle is referred to in a totally different way:

And David said unto Nathan, I have sinned against the LORD. And Nathan said unto David, The LORD also hath put away thy sin; thou shalt not die. Howbeit, because by this deed thou hast given great occasion to the enemies of the LORD to blaspheme, the child also that is born unto thee shall surely die... And it came to pass on the seventh day, that the child died... David perceived that the child was dead: therefore David said unto his servants, Is the child dead? And they said, He is dead. Then David arose from the earth, and washed, and anointed himself, and changed his apparel, and **came into the house of the LORD**, and worshipped: then he came to his own house; and when he required, they set bread before him, and he did eat. 2 Sam 12:13-20

Here it is called 'the house of the Lord'. It is a completely different Hebrew word which is rendered house. The word here is 'bayit' which means a dwelling place! How significant that the usage changes the description. The fact is that **all** of David's great encounters with God occurred **before** the construction of the Temple.

So was ended all the work that king Solomon made for the house of the LORD. And Solomon brought in the things which David his father had dedicated; even the silver, and the gold, and the vessels, did he put among the treasures of the house of the LORD...Then Solomon assembled the elders of Israel, and all the heads of the tribes, the chief of the fathers of the children of Israel, unto king Solomon in Jerusalem, that they might bring up the ark of the covenant of the LORD out of the city of David, which is Zion. 1 Kings 7:51; 8:1

It was fully 30 years after the passage in 2 Samuel above that the Temple was dedicated. (construction had begun in 1012BC and was finished in 1004 BC) The plain fact is that David didn't live to see the Temple built. He began the preparations for it but the Lord wouldn't allow him to begin the actual construction because he had 'blood on his hands'. He was allowed to bring the ark into the city, erect the tabernacle, and begin what we know as 'Davidic worship'. That speaks volumes about the great importance of the Tabernacle of David vis-à-vis the Temple. A pattern begins to come to light that revolutionizes the understanding of Davidic worship. There is much more involved in that process, both in spiritual significance and depth of meaning, than perhaps we have previously realized. Reading from the narrative of the erection of the Tabernacle of David gives us insight into the characteristics of that worship:

So they brought the ark of God, and set it in the midst of the tent that David had pitched for it: and they offered burnt sacrifices and peace offerings before God. And when David had made an end of offering the burnt offerings and the peace offerings, he blessed the people in the name of the LORD. And he dealt to every one of Israel, both man and woman, to every one a loaf of bread, and a good piece of flesh, and a flagon of wine. And he appointed certain of the Levites to minister before the ark of the LORD, and to record, and to thank and praise the LORD God of Israel: Asaph the chief, and next to him Zechariah, Jeiel, and Shemiramoth, and Jehiel, and

Mattithiah, and Eliab, and Benaiah, and Obededom: and Jeiel with psalteries and with harps; but Asaph made a sound with cymbals; Benaiah also and Jahaziel the priests with trumpets continually before the ark of the covenant of God. Then on that day David delivered first this psalm to thank the LORD into the hand of Asaph and his brethren. Give thanks unto the LORD, call upon his name, make known his deeds among the people. Sing unto him, sing psalms unto him, talk ye of all his wondrous works... Blessed be the LORD God of Israel for ever and ever. And all the people said, Amen, and praised the LORD. So he left there before the ark of the covenant of the LORD Asaph and his brethren, to minister before the ark continually, as every day's work required: And Obededom with their brethren, threescore and eight; Obededom also the son of Jeduthun and Hosah to be porters: And Zadok the priest, and his brethren the priests, before the tabernacle of the LORD in the high place that was at Gibeon, To offer burnt offerings unto the LORD upon the altar of the burnt offering continually morning and evening, and to do according to all that is written in the law of the LORD, which he commanded Israel; And with them Heman and Jeduthun, and the rest that were chosen, who were expressed by name, to give thanks to the LORD, because his mercy endureth for ever; And with them Heman and Jeduthun with trumpets and cymbals for those that should make a sound, and with musical instruments of God. And the sons of Jeduthun were porters. And all the people departed every man to his house: and David returned to bless his house. 1 Chron 16:1-9; 36-43

Let's examine these characteristics:

1] It was open to all as opposed to the Tabernacle of Moses in which only the priests could minister before the Lord – verse 1.

2] There was fellowship between God and man – verse 3.

3] As in the tabernacle of Moses there was the continual presence of the Lord – verse 4, verses 37-40, and verse 15:2.

4] There was continual music – verses 5-6 and verse 42.

5] There was worship and praise – verse 4 and verses 7-36.

6] There were offerings and service – verses 41-42.

Here David is reinstituting the original form of interaction with God in what scripture calls the Tabernacle of David. The ark rested under a simple tent and was open to all. Without realizing it David was creating a prophetic forerunner of the New Testament model of worship and ministry. When David entered Jerusalem, he wore a linen ephod – a priestly garment, assuming a king-priest role in the pattern of Melchisedec, and set in motion a chain of events that could have potentially restored the pre-Mosaic pattern of worship. But it was not to be. David desired to build a 'house' for God but the Lord rebuked him; once again human effort interrupted and replaced divine relationship. The fulfillment of the king-priest concept had to wait until the ministry of Jesus to be restored.

We then can take our cue from the pattern given here and use this 'recipe' for our own entry into the secret place. When Jesus talks of entering our closet we now know what he was referring to and what he intended for us to do about it. The concepts presented in this book are not new. They have always been there in scripture. We have only to enter in as David did (and as described in our two texts from Psalms) to enjoy the fulness of his presence in the secret place!

The *Deep Wells Collection* is a compilation of six mini-books, previously published separately as Kindle e-books. These small, power packed books cover a wide variety of subjects ranging from the parable of the ten virgins to the symbolic meanings of wind in scripture to what Jesus wore when he was resurrected. Each book is full of scripture references and will stimulate the reader's curiosity to draw from the 'deep wells' of God's wisdom. Blessed are those who hunger and **thirst**...

Available on Amazon – ISBN 978-1-947729-01-8

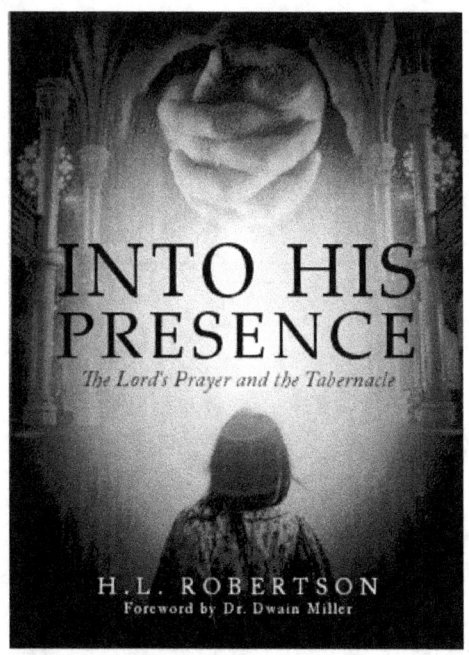

Into His Presence is a fresh and unique view of the Lord's Prayer. It is a phrase-by-phrase look at the most often repeated words ever spoken on this planet, combined with a step-by-step walk through of the Old Testament Tabernacle. Each phrase resonates with a part of the Old Testament worship process; showing that Jesus wasn't just teaching His followers a prayer to repeat, but that He was giving them a pathway to the intimate presence of His Father. His Jewish followers would have been closely acquainted with this type of worship, and as with so many of Jesus' teachings, would have understood these words on a far deeper level than most modern Christians would recognize. This book builds a framework of understanding for the reader, first of the Tabernacle worship system and then each phrase of the Lord's Prayer; explaining its meaning for us as believers and its significance in relation to the corresponding Tabernacle station. Also included in each chapter is a prayer of 'entering in' for that step in the journey.

Available on Amazon – ISBN 978-0-9987480-7-8

Sweet Aroma takes a unique viewpoint of the idea of our spiritual 'smell'. In this fascinating study, the author looks at the many scriptures dealing with this subject, including the aromas produced in the Tabernacle worship ceremonies, the stench of our fallen human nature in God's nostrils, and the extraordinary measures He took down through time to mask and cover our sin in order to pacify His holy anger toward us. Next, it investigates the concept of the blessing of the firstborn as first pictured in the story of Jacob and Esau; the role of Christ as the 'firstborn son', and the implications these principles have for us today. Finally it integrates these ideas into a framework for us to understand this revelation and to be able to proactively apply it to our everyday lives and our spiritual journey.

Available on Amazon – ISBN 978-0-9987480-6-1

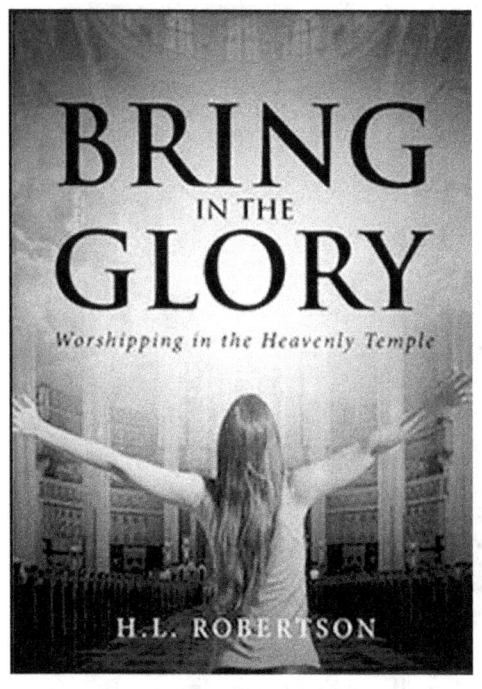

Have you ever tried to enter into worship only to 'hit a wall' and find you are unable to proceed deeper into God's presence and power? ***Bring in the Glory*** is an eye-opening look at both the worship process and the true dynamics of worship. It begins by establishing the concept of the heavenly temple and God's position in it. This is followed by an in depth study of the character and nature of worship in heaven; including its relationship to earthly worship, the role of the angels and the future role of the believers. It concludes with an examination of Davidic worship as a prophetic precursor to worship under the new covenant and the concept of pressing through the veil to bring the glory of God into our worship; both individually and corporately.

Available on Amazon – ISBN 978-0-9987480-8-5

www.ingramcontent.com/pod-product-compliance
Lightning Source LLC
Chambersburg PA
CBHW071528080526
44588CB00011B/1590